My Life Memories

James R. Bower

Copyright © 2023 James R. Bower

All rights reserved. No part of this book may be reproduced or transmitted in any form or by any means, electronic or mechanical, including photocopying, recording, or by any information storage and retrieval system without permission in writing from the publisher.

Average Dog Publishing–Deer Park, TX
Paperback ISBN: 978-1-7337590-8-3
Hardcover ISBN: 978-1-7337590-9-0
Library of Congress Control Number: 2023923502
Title: *My Life Memories*
Author: James R. Bower
Digital distribution | 2023 Paperback | 2023

My Memories

Born James R. Bower on September 13th, 1949 by what is called a Midwife in the small town of Clifford, Michigan.

Clifford is located in the thumb area about 90 miles north of Detroit. After I was born, my parents bought an 80-acre farm just outside of town. My dad cleared 40 acres of land for crops and left the other 40 acres for hunting and trapping.

We raised cattle, pigs, and chickens on the farm. Dad also planted large gardens to can and freeze for ourselves and to sell to others for extra money. Dad also worked at a grain elevator and would bring home corn that was ground up for corn meal mush for breakfast. With the meat, milk, vegetables, and corn meal, it saved on buying a lot of groceries during the week.

I was pretty small at the time and had no idea how rough it really was. We had an old outhouse quite a ways from the house. During the winter, it was quite a trip to it. For us kids, we had a covered pot up in our bedroom to use in the evening. We had an old hand pump mounted on the kitchen cabinet with a wash basin.

Our bedroom upstairs was freezing cold in the winter. Snow would blow through the window and cover the stairs. I remember having so many blankets on me I could barely roll over. I would keep my clothes under my covers to dress before I got out of bed. We had one small register on the floor above a coal/wood stove located in the living room below.

Behind that coal/wood stove in a corner is where we would take a bath. I still can't remember how my mother emptied that tub. It took a lot of hot water for her to fill it up.

I was about 4 years old when my parents noticed I had a problem with one of my eyes. My parents took me to the eye doctor and he sent us to a specialist.

The specialist (after a few 60-mile trips) wanted to operate and my dad said no. He took me back to the first doctor and he decided to put a patch over my good eye and watch fast-moving picture shows. Watching fast-moving shows with my bad eye would strengthen the muscles in it. It took some time, but I didn't need surgery on it. They called it "Lazy Eye."

I remember back then the doctors made house calls. My sister had gotten real sick and in order for the doctor to get to the house, he had to get a snow plow to get in front of him to break a trail. My parents bought an old oval-style TV in about 1951. I did miss the first year of school because of my eyes. I started school when I was 6 years old.

A few shows that I watched on that oval-styled TV are as follows:

Laurel and Hardy
The Three Stooges
Abbott and Castello
Disney
Adventures of Rin-Tin-Tin
Red Ryder
Sky King
The Lone Ranger
Roy Rogers
Gene Autry
Bozo the Clown
Poopdeck Paul – Popeyes and Pals
Looney Tunes
Mighty Mouse
Lawman
Gunsmoke
Have Gun Will Travel
Wanted Dead or Alive
Tales of Wells Fargo
Combat
Cheyenne
And many more.

I was 5 years old when my tonsils burst. I can still remember seeing that black mask coming down over my face with the ether to put me to sleep. When I got home, I found out my parents had bought me a tricycle.

It didn't last three days because I left it behind my Dad's car.

The first car that I remember my parents having was a 1950 Ford. The back doors wouldn't stay shut so my Dad tied a rope from handle to handle to keep the doors shut.

The eye doctor had my eyes corrected with glasses by the time I started school. My school was just down the street from where my dad worked. There was a low rail fence dividing where he worked and the place next door. While waiting for my dad, I would walk that rail. I slipped one day, fell, and broke my glasses in two pieces.

He wasn't too thrilled but he took me to get a new pair at the eye doctor's office. The eye doctor was located behind the hardware store that my dad wanted to go to next. He had a hold of my hand and I was following him. I saw something across the street and I was walking backward. When I turned around, I ran straight into a parking meter, and like before, I broke my new glasses in two pieces.

This is about the time I started drawing. I did a lot of drawing back then. We didn't have a lot of money back then, so I would cut up grocery bags and use them to draw on. My mother would draw and paint so I was pretty sure that's what I would do. I have quite a few copies of her drawings.

While walking home from school. I would

sometimes stop at the telephone building and watch the switchboard operator answer the phones. She would have to plug and unplug the cables while answering the calls. The first phone that I remember my parents having was a wood box-type with a crank to ring the operator.

My mom would order our school clothes through the Sears and Robach catalog. My little sister and I were walking home from school when a neighbor stopped to give us a ride home. He stopped on the road to let us out and as I was thanking him, I heard tires squealing. Someone had hit my sister. She had to have a body cast for 9 months.

Way back by our woods was a tall hill full of hardwoods. Some of the hardwood trees had initials carved in them from long ago. In these woods were huge rocks that I used to like to climb and sit on. Sitting on this rock in the warm sun and being able to see for a long way was a great feeling.

One winter, the snow got so deep that my brothers had to jump out of the upstairs window so they could shovel the snow away from the door so we could get out.

Living on the farm, we had to get up early to feed the animals and milk the cow before we got ready for school. After school, the animals had to be fed, cow to milk, garden to be weeded, fields to be worked. In the summers, my brothers and I would work for other farmers. We had two hunting dogs, one was a beagle and one was a pointer.

When other hunters showed up with their dogs, the beagle would start a fight and then go lie down to watch the pointer finish the fight.

My mom used to smoke and as a curious kid, I had to try some of the cigarette butts she left. My dad caught me out by the barn with them.

All he said was if I wanted to smoke, do it at the house. He didn't want me to burn the barn down. Dad then told me if I smoked, It had to be cigars. My mom didn't take it too lightly. I smoked cigarettes, cigars, and pipes until I was 22 years old and then I got smart and quit smoking.

I went to Marlette High School. I started there in the ninth grade. I didn't get a chance to do sports because of farm work. In my 12th-grade year, I only needed to take a government class. The rest of the day, I went to work in a tool and die shop. I started classes at Norman Rockwells' "Famous Artist School" but I never got to finish because of going into the military.

My first girlfriend lived in another town. Our parents were best of friends, so we practically grew up together. She went to college and I went into the military. We both ended up marrying someone else. The four of us stayed in touch. To this day, we are still best of friends. When I graduated, my graduation and going away party were the same party.

During my training, I developed heat exhaustion that turned into Spinal meningitis. The army flew my parents to where I was in the hospital and got them a place to stay. When I finally got out of the hospital, they sent me home for 30 days and then I had to report to a rehabilitation center before going back into training.

I had to finish training and to see if I could make it, I signed up for airborne infantry. I received my orders for my A.I.T. unit. Five other guys and I went through special training. We were trained to know all the weapons used in Vietnam and went to Demolition Training. We were trained by the South Vietnamese so we could train our troops.

I received my orders for Jump School. That was a tough school. If I had not made it, I wouldn't have tried it again. Luckily, all was good and I passed. Nobody had rank at the time, only the Black Hats were in charge. I received my orders after graduation from Jump School to go to my new unit, the 82nd Airborne.

When I first arrived, there, things started happening. They put barbed wire around the buildings and the doors were chained shut. We couldn't send mail, payphones were off-limits. We had to go to the armory and pick up our weapons. They didn't let us know until later what was happening.

It was January 1969, if I remember correctly in December 1968, the North Koreans captured one of our ships, The "Pueblo," so we geared up and got on the plane under "Operation Focus Retna." We stopped and fueled up in Alaska, and from there, we landed in Okinawa. We left there, put our parachutes on while flying, and jumped into Korea out of the C-141 Jets.

It was February then, cold and freezing rain. That was my first jump with the 82nd. Most of the time was spent training others and fighting riots. My unit trained ROTC cadets, West Point cadets, and Special Forces. We fought riots in Connecticut and Washington D.C.

I volunteered for Vietnam three times, feeling I wasn't doing my part, but each time I was told that I was more valuable in the States than I would be there. The last few months I was in, I got to go to architectural school before I got out, which helped me with a job outside of the military.

I was offered a rank of E-6 and a $10,000 bonus to re-up but turned it down. The last year that I was in the army, I got married. I finally got out in June of 1971. My son was born in September of 1971.

I got a job with a real estate company remodeling houses for $3.00 an hour. There were other jobs on the houses in different areas, which going back and forth at the time would eat up my wages in gas. There were three other guys on the crew and they decided that one day they wanted to go hunting instead of going to work.

I couldn't handle what we were doing by myself, so I stayed home. The boss showed up at my house and fired me, the best thing that could have happened. I don't know what happened to the other guys, never saw them again. I ended up getting hired into a modular home factory. I started out working on the line building the homes.

One day I was punching the clock and saw a notice on the board that they needed a Draftsman in their engineering department. The next day, I talked to my foreman about it and he sent me to fill out an application for the job. I finally got to talk to the manager and landed the job. I started out as a print runner.

After a while, I started making corrections on drawings until I finally worked my way up on drawings until I finally worked my way up to be a designer. Later, I got to do design work on my brother's house that he ordered, and also designed my own home and had it built. I worked there for 10 years for a whopping $3.50 an hour.

There were a few months when I was laid off that I worked for a motor home factory until I was called back to the home factory. During that time, my daughter was born and we were living in a farm home that we were renting. The modular home that we had built was a 3 bedroom sitting on a full basement. We had the well drilled and septic system and did it all for $22,000.

After a few years, we sold the modular house and bought a house in the next town that was built in 1861. The house was actually a stagecoach stop. It had 20 rooms and sat on 3/12 acres in the middle of town. After a few years, we sold that home and rented a house in another town. We stayed there until the housing went down and everyone was being let go at the factory.

I contacted my sister who lived in Texas and she started sending me the want ads. I showed one to my boss and he said to check on that one because at one time, they wanted to hire him.

I went to Texas to check on a few ads. I got there on a Saturday and bought a newspaper to check the ads. That place still had the ad for a chief designer. I went there on Monday to apply and they wanted me to start right then. We hadn't even moved yet. They moved us and I started a couple of weeks later. I stayed at the job for 10 years.

During that time, everything was turning to electronics. I was still drawing on the drawing board and everything was changing to computers. I knew eventually if I didn't go back to school, I would be forced out of a job. I contacted the college to sign up and took a computer-aided drafting class, along with computer basics.

The company had already purchased a couple of computers but wanted to hire experienced operators to use them. Finally, I just moved all my stuff over to them and started using them until I switched jobs.

Just as we moved to Texas, the "Urban Cowboy Seen" was on. With Mickey Gilly's Club and Johnny Lee's Club just down the road from us, my wife wanted to be there. I'm not a crowd or party person. She went with her friends and I stayed with the kids. It finally ended our marriage and I got my kids.

I had a boy and a girl and one of my co-workers had two girls and a boy. I would ask her about taking care of my daughter and she would ask me questions about taking care of her son. Eventually, we got together and got married.

We lived in an apartment for a while and then started looking for a house. It was tough because my divorce left me bankrupt and my wife's divorce left her with no credit. We found a little house that a doctor's wife had bought and fixed up because she wanted to work in real estate.

Even though we figured we had no chance, we filled out some loan applications. The next day, we got a phone call saying we were approved. The doctor and his wife financed us themselves. One day, I got a phone call from the doctor saying we needed to have a meeting about the financing.

I thought he was going to raise our payments. He explained that the house payments were putting him into a high tax bracket, so he lowered our payments and reduced how many years we had to pay. Shortly after, we paid the house off and decided to look for a weekend getaway place. Finally found a place about 2½ hours away out in the country.

There was a mobile home, a barn, a pond, a well, and a septic on 10 acres.

They took the mobile home so we purchased a modular home and put it on the concrete slab that was there. As I was building fences around the place a herd of longhorns from another ranch got out. They caught all but one. I caught the other one and found out who she belonged to.

I eventually bought her from the guy and she ended up having a calf so I ended up getting two for the price of one. We ended up buying 5 more head of cattle and then applied for the agriculture tax exemption.

I spent every weekend for 3 years building fences.

My neighbor was an actual cowboy. Before he retired, he was the foreman of three 4,000-acre ranches where they actually had to use horses for the cattle. He sold me one of his horses whose name was "Blackjack." We bought another horse that turned out to be mean so we sold him and later on, we bought a beautiful paint named Charlie. Charlie was an Ex-Police horse and he loved everyone.

Out there were wild hogs and the people around there hunted them with dogs. They would practically starve them to make them hunt. The dogs would get loose and kill my calves. I learned that ranchers would run donkeys with their cattle for protection because donkeys didn't like dogs.

I found a donkey for sale and went and bought her. Later on, she had a little one. Again, I got two for the price of one. Our weekend place got to be a full-time job so I had to hire a couple to take care of it during the week. I ended up having to build 3 more barns to handle all of the equipment and to feed the animals.

We then decided to raise buffalo and I located a small herd. That led to building stronger fences and pens. I divided the place so the bison was on one side and the cattle and horses were on the other side.

Since we had to find a bull for our small herd of bison, I finally found one about 100 miles away. He was huge and weighed about 2,000 pounds. We got him in the trailer and he was bouncing both the truck and trailer up and down. He tore the center gate out of the trailer, and we lost the axles off from under the trailer just as we got back to the ranch.

During that time, we found a building for

sale in the town square. We thought we would like to turn it into an old-fashioned ice cream parlor when we retired. In the meantime, we leased it to the county to store their equipment in.

One day, a tornado hit and took the roof of the building next to us and dropped it on top of our building. The county took their equipment out of our building and canceled their lease. One day, a couple of guys wanted to lease it and turn it into a restaurant.

I told them that's fine but I'm not putting any money into it. They got someone to back them. Now we had that to take care of also. The same guy who took care of our ranch also took care of the restaurant during the week. Our house was in need of repair because all my time was spent on the ranch.

We talked it over and decided to find another house. We bought another house and it was farther away from the ranch than the other one was. We decided we needed to do things with the grandkids so we bought this huge motor home and we kept it at the ranch.

We made trips to the Yogi Bear Park and water parks. One day we were talking about motorcycles because I used to ride them. She was really against them because she thought they were too dangerous.

We were having lunch one day just next

door to the Harley Davidson dealer. I suggested we just look around because we weren't in a hurry. Just as we walked in, there sat a beautiful blue metal flaked, triglide trike. The salesman talked her into sitting on it, and we ended up buying it. She loved it. We rode it out west and went to South Dakota to the Sturgis Rally.

We rode all through the Black Hills. We had a toy hauler that the back end turned into a garage for the bike.

After retiring in 2017, I got back into my artwork. I had a studio built in my backyard with a covered walkway and deck onto it. I got to know Chuck Norris after doing his portrait for him.

Going through some of my old drawings, I found a comic strip of my old dog Spike. I tried getting it into the newspapers way back about 40 years ago. I drew them and decided to try and send them to book publishers. One of the publishers liked it so the first book was published. At this time, I have 7 books published plus this one coming up next and another in process.

I'm the president of the Deer Park Art League.

Since getting back into my art and writing/illustrating my books that are worldwide, I've come in contact with hundreds of artists from all over the world.

It's been an amazing trip.

As of now, my wife and I have 5 children, 16

grandchildren, and 9 great grand-children.

My memories end here because my wife passed away in March of 2023.

The home I grew up in.

Me, my two brothers, and my sister in the back. Two of my cousins in the front.

My grade school.

My high school.

June of 1968, the day I left for the army.

Airborne training photo.

Standing on a friend's porch in North Carolina.

One of our jumps.

The type of gun jeeps I was squad leader of (106 re-coilless rifle with 50 cal mounted on top)

One of the houses I had in Michigan.

My office at the modular home factory.

My office in the building factory in Houston.

The next pages are of our ranch.

Our first motorhome

Our second motorhome

Our toy hauler

Our bike rides

The boss dog and I

Our Mexican restaurant out by the ranch.

Our home in Deer Park, Texas.

My art studio behind our house.

The characters in my children's books.
Socks, Boss, and Spike.

Carlotta and I
1985

Carlotta and I
2023

About the Author

James R. Bower, retired designer of architectural and mechanical engineering. A U.S. paratrooper, veteran of the '60s and 70's. The president of the Deer Park Art League in Deer Park, Texas

www.ingramcontent.com/pod-product-compliance
Lightning Source LLC
Chambersburg PA
CBHW061741070526
44585CB00024B/2769